Flash Fiction
Short Stories

Volume 1

By
Judi Wallower

2

Dedication

This is dedicated to Jacob and Jenna.
I love you more than the sky is high.

4

Awake At the Wake

Note To Self

Playground Memories

Please Don't

Silence Isn't Golden

The Gumshoe

The Humble Award

Welcome To the Neighborhood

6

Awake At the Wake

Someone is touching me, why are there so many people around me. Why am I wearing an oxygen mask…and an IV. What the hell happened?

"Hey! Somebody. I'm ok. Please get off me."

Why can't they hear me? I can't seem to move. There are so many wires on me, and I'm being loaded into an ambulance, and they are moving quickly, oh, that's not a good sign.

Last thing I remember is…I was riding my bike in the city marathon, and someone was being chased, ran into me, and knocked me off my bike. Oh, my head is killing me.

Heart monitor leads are on my chest, and I hear beeping. They are talking so fast. I feel cold.

"He's in shock. BP is 60/20 and heartrate is 176. IV fluids are administered. ETA is two minutes. Drive faster, we're losing him."

'Losing him.' Who is he talking about? Not me. It can't be me. I don't want to die.

"Hey dude! I don't want to die! Help me. Do you hear me. Please help me!"

The beeps are slowing. What's going on? Oh, no!

Beep…Beep…….Beeeeeeeppp……

"He's in Vfib! Starting CPR." The EMT is saying as the ambulance pulls up to the double doors to the emergency room. The rescue doors open with people dressed in yellow personal protective coats over their scrubs, reaching out and grabbing the gurney out of the rescue and swiftly enter trauma bay 3. Everyone is running and everyone is working simultaneously. It's overwhelming.

"No pulse."

"Charge defibrillator to 200."

"Clear!"

"No pulse."

"Charge to 300."

"Clear!"

"Nothing."

"Charge to 360."

"Clear!"

"Nothing." The nurse says as she looks at the doctor with sad eyes.

"Starting CPR."

"Dr. Dr. He's gone. He was gone before he arrived. I'm sorry."

"T.O.D. 3:44 p.m. "The attending doctor says ripping off his gloves and throwing them on the floor and storming out of the trauma room.

****

Uh. Now where am I? I must have fallen asleep, the last thing I remember is being in the ambulance. I must be ok, right? Why is it so quiet and dark in here…and cold, and hard…metal-like. Is that a sheet on my face? Why? Where are the doctors and nurses.

Oh, ok. I heard someone coming in. They are pulling the sheet off my face. Ah, that's better, at least I can see now.

"Hey. Hey Doc, help me. What's going on? Where am I?"

Why is she ignoring me? She's not even looking at me and where are my clothes?

"Dr. Erica Robins, today is May 10, 2023, performing the autopsy of Michael Richard Thompson, thirty-three years of age. Died May 9, 2023, of head trauma from a fall off a bicycle. Cutting the Y incision….."

Autopsy! Me? Am I? Am I…dead? OMG! No! I can't believe it. I can hear everything that's going on. I can feel her touching me…poking and prodding me like I'm a pork chop. OMG, could that be why she isn't answering me? But I can't be dead. I'm still alive! I'm still alive!

****

Now where am I? Why do I keep fading in and out? I'm in some other room now. Why can't anyone see that I'm still alive? I am not dead…I can't be dead.

Here comes another guy. Now where am I? He's spraying my eyes, nose, and mouth. Now he's shaving my face. Hey buddy, I can shave my own face thank you…or I used to anyway.

He's gluing my mouth, giving me a massage, and oh, I feel a strange sensation throughout my body, my… Oh, no. I know what's happening, I must be in the mortuary. Well, I guess this is real. I AM dead.

****

Hhhmm. I smell flowers and…coffee. Oh, thank God it was all just a bad dream. Oh, I'm so glad. It was just a Jacob Marley dream. It smells great downstairs. Aw, she's so sweet to make me coffee before leaving this morning. 7 a.m. She must have gotten up early this morning. God bless her heart. I have a feeling it's going to be a wonderful day today.

****

What time is it? It's dark again. I must have fallen back to sleep. Ok, why are my legs stiff. Why can't I move? Something is wrong. I'm scared after that dream I had…it was so real. I better get her to take me to the E.R.

I'm yelling for her. Why isn't she answering? She's not coming, and I don't hear anything. Oh, no. She's not home. No, she needs to be home. I need her. I need her now and she's not hearing me.

Uh, wait. I hear someone. Oh good. She's coming. She's pulling up the shades.

Wait, what?

Where am I? Who are you? HEY! What the hell is going on? This can't be real…it was all just a dream, right?

I can't move and I can only see peripherally. Someone is approaching. Who is that guy and why is he in my house and wearing a suit? Where is she? I need her right now.

Ahh, thank God. She's here. She and mom are crying and looking down on me. Down?

Hey, I'm here. Can't you hear me? Help me get out of here. Please! Help me! Wait, I can see…casket? I'm in a casket? Am I? I'm not…dead? I can't be dead. Am I having another dream?

Oh my God! I AM DEAD! How can that be? I am in a funeral home. I don't want to dead.

No. No. No. That can't be. Oh my God. Am I crying? I can't tell.

I'm hearing chatter. There's my brother and sister-in-law. There are my aunts and uncles. They're all crying.

The last thing I remember is I was in the city marathon and… Somebody!

Boy, I can hear everything crystal clear. Everyone's conversations, even the people way in the back of the room. I guess you get special powers when you die. Die? No. I don't want powers...I want to be alive.

Now, who is that girl? I don't recognize her. Here she comes. Oh. That's my ex-girlfriend. Ha. Why is she even here? That was from 7 or 8 years ago. I can't believe she's so upset. We barely dated. She was obsessive and then after three months she dumped me for some beefy guy with no IQ. She's blonde now. She needs another dye job. Haha.

Aw, there is my old neighbor from growing up. She was always so sweet. She used to bake us cookies all the time. Ended up having all the neighborhood kids at her house. Word got around and she would have to bake 4 dozen cookies just to feed all of us.

Oh, crap. Are you kidding me. I can't believe *he* came. He had me fired from my job. He's as ruthless as they come. We were both up for the same promotion and I heard from the grapevine that I had a decent chance of getting it.

Well, one day he screwed up an account and pinned it on me. Well, I didn't get the promotion, the promotion went to him, and I got fired after speaking up about it. Told me I was jealous. Jerk-off. I was next in line for it, I worked hard, and I deserved it.

Now he's here at my wake. Two-faced hypocrite. Get away from my wife jerk!

Oh my God! Boy did she get fat! I can't believe it's her. Oh, no. She's getting too close to the casket. She's putting something in with me. No! Don't lean on it. No, stop shaking it. I'm going to fall. You're going to make me fall out. How embarrassing. Stop, just leave it. It doesn't have to be perfect.

Shew. That was close. I thought for sure I was going overboard.

DING-A-BLING......DING-A-BLING......DING-A-BLING

Oh, no. It's over already. No. I still don't know why I died. Was it like in the dream, someone pushed me off my bike at the marathon? Not anyone spoke of my unfortunate ending. I need to know.

NO. Don't go. Stop. Get away from my casket. Don't close it. NO. Please don't.........NOOOOO!!

Uh. Uh. What's happening? I hear muffled voices, crying, and.... music?

Wait.

The casket is moving again. Voices are getting softer and farther away. This can't be happening to me. My life cannot be over.

****

Jolting to a sitting position, sweat pouring down my face, panting to catch my next breath, and my heart palpitating.

Oh, my God. If that's not the worst dream I ever had. Wow. That was intense. I need coffee.

Heading into the kitchen, I see and smell the coffee that she made. I assume she left. She usually leaves for work before I do.

14

Sitting at the table with my cup and newspaper…yes…I still read the actual newspaper. Ahhhh.

What a beautiful day this is going to be. This is the best cup of coffee I ever had.

My throat feels funny suddenly, like it's tightening. It's burning. I hope I am not getting sick. Ugh, it's so bad now and my stomach is on fire. I'm going to throw up, but I don't think I'm going to make it to the bathroom. What's happening? My body is on fire and convulsing and white liquid foaming out of my mouth.

I look up to see her standing over me grinning. I am unable to speak, and my eyesight is blurring. Why? Why would she do this to me. I treated you like gold, I thought we were happy.

OMG! There he was standing next to her looking down at me. He turned to look at her and kissed her. He kissed her! It's that jerk-off from my old job. NOOOOOO!

She looks at me and says, "Goodbye Charlie. See you later."

And those are the last words I ever heard.

15

Note to Self

Dear Self,

I know I didn't always make the right life choices, but that's in the past and the past cannot be changed no matter how hard I wish for it.

I wasn't the most responsible, I spent money I did not have, I borrowed money from people who I knew I wasn't going to pay back. I bought beer for underage kids thinking I was cool, and I didn't care what happened.

I took partying to the very limits, drinking all I could every weekend. Challenged others to drinking contests until we passed out and put others' lives in danger.

I ignored what was the most important…my family. Not attending family functions, not having any money left to buy birthday or Christmas presents for mom, dad, or sister. Not being there for my sister when she was fatally sick, and I could never get that time back.

I wasn't always the most upstanding citizen, I got in trouble with the law, and I thought I was swift, and I would shoot my mouth off to the police officer and end up going to jail. I was disrespectful.

I bullied and played jokes on the most vulnerable people and laughed about it.

I'm guessing…no I know all these things are why I am stuck in life. Stuck without happiness or having things that most people have begun achieving at my age…late twenties. Am I being punished for my prior bad actions? Does karma play a role in life? Some believe in that sort of thing, I never used to…until now. I sure do.

So, self, today, I acknowledge my past person which I cannot change, but can learn from. Yesterday was my wake-up call. I saw a situation unfold right in front of me. A hold-up at the local liquor store by a young man in his early twenties who robbed the store at gunpoint, I was there when it all went down.

Someone inside the store called the police. Did I take out my phone and call the police? No. I froze. I hid in the back like a coward. Panicking, I accidentally kicked a can of soup off the shelf and the robber heard it, grabbed me by the arm, and threw me down on the floor with the other hostages.

The police arrived and were negotiating for a peaceful settlement to the situation, but the robber didn't want any part of it and remained inside the store waving his gun in all directions. The man was rattled and becoming unhinged with every minute that past.

The police were outside still trying to get through to the robber to release us, the hostages and give himself up but it wasn't working. He didn't want to go to jail. He was disheveled and sweating like a flowing creek.

We were in there for hours but felt like days. Then the man made his move.

He grabbed me by my arms once again holding a gun to my head…hoping to get away I suppose. He proceeded to drag me towards the front door. I've never been so scared in all my life. What if the police start shooting. They don't know we are coming out.

"Open the door!" He yelled at me.

"Stay back or I will kill him!"

"Son, put the gun down, you don't want to kill anyone. It will only make things worse for you. Let's settle this calmly and we can help you out of this," the police said to him as all guns were focused.

What if this turns horribly bad. I could be dead in an instant.

"Get back. I just want a car and get away," he said. "Do it or I'll kill him."

I began to shake and feel weak, and I wanted to throw up.

"Release the hostage and we can make that happen, but we can't let you take him with you."

"No. I won't let him go, he's my insurance policy."

"I give you my word, we won't harm you,"

"Hold your fire! Hold your fire!" Captain Chase yelled out to his men.

"Ok, son. Raise your hands over your head nice and slowly."

And with that, a team of SWAT with bulletproof shields swarmed over the robber, grabbed the gun in his hand, and guided him down to the ground to handcuff him, while simultaneously another team of SWAT grabbed me and took me to safety.

A police car took him to jail, and an ambulance transported me and all the other hostages to the hospital to get checked out.

Afterwards, I slept the days away, my family grew concerned and I started going to therapy and I must say, it was the best wake-up call I could have ever gotten. It made me rethink my life and realize the jerk I have been. I hurt many people, and I cannot take that back, but I can try to apologize to those and move forward to create a better life for myself and for the people that surround me. The people that surround me with love and support and still care about me even though I made their lives somewhat miserable.

That day, innocent people got dragged into a scary situation made by a man who made bad choices.

Two men…both making bad choices…both had their lives changed forever. One man goes to jail while the other changes his life for the good.

I pledge to change for the good and overcome my prior self and make a promising future for myself.

So, what do I want for my future self? I want a decent job…a career. A job that I will enjoy, a job that I will be good at. I promise to be diligent, loyal, respectful, and focused. I will be carefully selective in my choice, learn, work hard, and become educated in that field so I can be the best self I can be.

To have a job that will make me successful within the industry as well as financially secure. I don't want to struggle for the things I need and to be able to acquire things and have fun and be entertained. To be able to build savings for retirement years and hopefully for my future family. And, to have the ability to help those who can't help themselves and donate to charity when I can.

A home of my own with lots of land to hang and entertain in, a pool would be cool for the summer months, a garage I can use for my hobby of woodworking. I enjoy making things from wood whether it is plaques, hanging baskets for plants, bookshelves, and more. I can create projects for myself and give creations to others and make them smile.

Family. A wife I adore and who loves me, kids running around. A family who would rely on me to take care of them, provide for them, love them, make them laugh with my dumb daddy jokes. A family who I can teach all about life, how to fix things, how to build with wood. A family I can take to the movies, teach them bowling, and discipline them when they need it so they can grow up into strong, loving, educated adults. A family is priceless. I realize this now.

Future self, I know this seems like a long and unattainable list but let me assure you by saying I know I can do it. I am growing, learning to overcome my past mistakes, and I am dreaming of a future. A positive future, one I could be proud of and proud to pass along to my children as well as to others.

I would like to become a mentor and pay forward what I have experienced and what I have become so that I can help other People need to know that they are not alone, there are many people who are like me and if I can help them through their situation, would make me happy knowing I helped make someone's life better.

So, future self, I begin this journey…the good road. It doesn't matter when I started, the important thing is that I have. It's not going to be easy…I know this…life is full of curve balls and rollercoasters, and I am proud to be experiencing the journey of life.

Love,

Me

23

Playground Memories

"Hi. My name is Kyle. What's your name?"

"Hi. I'm Cari. I just moved here."

"Is that your mom over there?"

"Yeah."

"She's talking to my mom."

"Oh."

"Do you like it here?"

"It's ok. My mom said we had to move on account of my mom and dad split up."

"Oh. That sucks. Hey, but it's nice here in Hightown. What grade will you be going in when the summer is over?

"Fourth grade."

"Hey me too. Maybe we will be in the same class. That way you won't feel alone, you'll have me."

"That would be fun."

"Do you have a pool at your new house?"

"No, not yet, but my mom said we can get one next summer."

"Maybe you and your mom can come over our house one day and swim in our pool, since we know each other now and our moms' are friends."

"That's awesome. Thanks Kyle."

"Sure. Let's go play on the monkey bars."

"Ok."

****

"So, Corrine. How long have you been living here?"

"Well, A.J. is it?"

"Yes. It's short for Andrea Jean."

"Well, A.J., it's been about a month. Just long enough to unpack everything and sign Cari up for school. I wanted to get her school taken care of so we can get to know the area over the summer. This is the first day we had to relax."

"Oh, I know how that feels," A.J. says waving her hands.

"Oh, did you move here recently too?"

"A couple years ago. I caught my husband cheating, got a great lawyer, cleaned him out. I sold the house and moved here to

Hightown to make a clean start. Kyle is happier, the schools are much better, and the area is charming."

"I'm sorry to hear that, but it's good Kyle is doing so well. You never know how kids will handle going through something like this."

"Oh, dear. I'm not sorry. It was the best thing for both of us. I thought I was in love with Kyle's father, I got pregnant, but we were doomed from the start. We tried to make it work, but he couldn't stop looking around, ya know."

"I like the area so far, it's nice and everything is close by, the people are friendly, and this playground is awesome."

They both paused their conversation to check on their kids. They were running around the playground laughing loudly and finally settled on the roundabout, jumped on to take the last two spaces. They were having a blast, as if they had always known each other.

"Well, it looks like our kids have already decided we were going to be friends," said as they both smiled.

A.J. stands up looking to get the kids' attention.

"Kyle! Cari!"

"Yeah mom!"

"Both of you come here for a minute," she says as she waves them over.

"Aw, do we have to leave now?

"No, Kyle. I just want you to sit for a minute and stay hydrated," she said as she hands the kids two small bottles of water.

"Hi Kyle. I'm Corrine, Cari's mom," she holds out her hand and Kyle gently shakes.

"And my name is A.J. My, aren't you just adorable."

"Thank you."

"Cari, how are you liking it here so far? Are you having fun on the playground with Kyle?"

"Oh yes. It's way fun."

"Sweetie, maybe you and Kyle will be in the same class in school."

"Yeah, Kyle already told me. Can we go back and play now?"

"Yes. Go. Have a blast."

"Ok. Can we get ice cream later mom? Please mom?" Kyle asks.

"We'll see. Go play."

"Ok," he says as they run to the roundabout again.

****

"Corrine, have you found work yet?"

"I put in a few applications, but I haven't found anything yet."

"Well, I have an offer for you if you're interested. A couple of years ago, I started a real estate company. I will pay you to get your realtors license and come work for me. It's just me and Jackie, my assistant. The business is growing, and I could use another realtor. I had to turn away some clients and I don't like to do that. It's a great industry, fun, and it pays well. I enjoy helping people find their forever home. What do you say?"

"A.J., that sounds perfect. Thank you so much. But are you sure, I mean, we just met?"

"We have been sitting here talking for two hours and our kids are having a blast, so, I'd say that qualifies. I think it will work out great. I have a good intuition about these things."

"Yeah, we can't deny the looks on their faces. I haven't seen Cari this happy since before we got here. The split with her father has been difficult for her. She doesn't see or communicate with her dad often. It's the main thing we have been fighting about lately."

"I completely understand. I am lucky in that way…it's the only thing Kyle's father and I do agree on is raising our son and he lives close enough that Kyle can see his dad anytime."

"My main reason for moving to Hightown is that it's a great family area…Cari is my first priority."

"Absolutely. Same here."

Eight Years Later

"Hey Cari. Come here a second."

"Yeah, what's up?"

"Remember when we first met when we were kids. You and your mom just moved here. You were sitting on these swings looking so sad."

"Ha-Ha. Yeah. I was so upset about everything happening…then you came along."

"That was the best thing that ever happened to me," Kyle smiles.

"Yeah. And look at us now."

"Yeah. A lot has happened to both our families. Moving here was the best thing for all of us. Both our mom's got remarried and are very happy. Your mom had a baby. Everything is great."

"Next week we graduate high school. I can't believe it."

"And then we go to the Harris County Community College in the fall. Me for nursing and you for criminal justice and then you go off to the police academy."

"Yeah, I can't wait for that…I mean, of course I'll miss you. But I'll be back as Officer Kyle Griffin. Pretty cool right. But the academy is not right away, we'll be in college first."

"Yeah. I am looking forward to college too. Learning all I can about nursing and possibly going further if I wanted to later, maybe be a doctor. I can't wait to treat people and help them feel better. Like what you did for me."

Kyle and Cari smile at each other.

"Kyle. You're the best thing that happened to me too. I love you."

"I love you too Cari."

They kiss.

"I have been wanting to say that for a really long time," Kyle said. "I loved you since the day we met. I knew when we got along that day on this playground that we were going to be friends for life."

"You bring out the best in me," Cari smiles.

"I'll bet if we jump off the swings, I can land further than you."

"Bet you can't."

<u>Epilogue</u>

"Gabriella! Dane! Junior! Stay together please!" A.J. said to her young grandchildren.

"Mom, this was a great idea to have a picnic at the playground," Cari said.

"Well, today is the anniversary of when we all met. You met Kyle and I met A.J., and we became a family. It seemed only fitting for all of us to come here and celebrate. I thought the kids would enjoy it and we can make some new playground memories."

"So many remarkable things have come from our chance meeting. You and Kyle are married and gave us three terrific grandchildren, I met and married Brian," A.J. said.

"And if it weren't for our moving here, I would not have met Jon, and we have Jon Jr. I am extremely happy with our family," said Corrine as she looked around at everyone.

"Besides, it gives us a chance to see our three adorable grandkids," A.J. said.

"Mom, you see the kids all the time," Kyle said.

"Yes, and we love every single minute."

Please Don't

"Please don't do it. Don't leave and go off somewhere. Your state of mind is not stable right now, and I know you are hurting…your perception of things are the absolute worst, but the grass isn't always greener. The grass is green where and what you make of it.

I fear that if you leave, you will end up on a bad path or worse. It may seem like the only option now…give up…to leave…but that could lead to an unsafe path which could be difficult to come back from if you do at all.

I'm not trying to put you down…I know you are smart. What I'm saying is that you are trusting, and have a huge heart, I would hate to see anyone take advantage of you in any way. I love you so much and hate to see you hurting.

If you stay, I will help you in every way I can…we all will. We can help find you someone to talk to, we can help find your in-house treatment if that's what makes you comfortable.

Don't worry about how…we will figure it out and we will make it happen. I don't want you to worry about the details, all I want you to focus on is getting better. You are a strong person and have been thrown a curve ball in your life, I understand you aren't used to feeling this way. Take the first step and you can begin your journey to happiness.

It's not going to be easy, but you have a great support system and I have every confidence you can heal and look towards a wonderful future.

Running away from your problems won't make them go away, they will only follow you. The best way to deal with them is to face your problems and fears. You are stronger than you think you are. You can beat this.

Now I see the look on your face, you look so sad, and you doubt yourself. I understand why you would feel that way, I was there when we thought we had lost you. I know things can be better but always remember that things can always be much worse.

Now I know it doesn't seem fair and it isn't, but life isn't always fair. We all have various levels of situations in our lives and what is effective, what makes us stronger with each situation is how we manage them. Everyone is not the same, so you can't look at other situations.

Please don't misunderstand me, I sound harsh, and it can be a rough climb up this mountain, and you are thinking that it's impossible, but it's not. It's totally possible. I know you can do it…you are stronger than you realize, and we will be with you along the way. Baby steps. I know I repeat that you are strong, but it's true.

I have been doing all the talking and I want to hear from you. What are you feeling? What do you want to do to get well? What do you want for your future? Yes, you can still have a productive life. Talk about anything you want and afterwards we will design a plan for you.

Don't be embarrassed, I am not here to judge you. No one should judge anyone, no one is perfect, and everyone has demons, skeletons, and embarrassing issues in their lives, they just don't always announce them. People like to talk and point out all the good things in their lives, making others feel like everything is perfect, but no one's life is perfect. They have the bad with the good like everyone else does. Don't let anyone else's life make you feel bad."

****

"Yeah, ok. I hear you yet I am skeptical. I find it hard to talk about myself, I don't know how to express my feelings, but I will give it a shot. I don't know where to start because everything is garbled in my head and spinning like a pinwheel. I am devastated, and I can't make sense of it. I was completely blindsided.

My accident nearly killed me, and my wife left me because of this wheelchair. It's all too much to bear. So, I don't see how I can get my life back, any life. I don't feel like me anymore.

Yes, the doctor said it's possible I can walk again, yet it's possible I won't walk again. I have seen videos of people going through physical therapy who have lost their ability to walk, I'm not as strong as they are. I feel it's a waste of time for me to just find out in the end that PT isn't working, and I'll be in this chair for the rest of my life.

Because of this accident I lost the job that I loved. I don't have money…I don't have a wife and I don't have a life.

You asked me what I want for my future…I want my old life back. I know that's impossible. So, I ask you what kind of future can I have?

So, you plead for me not to leave but being around here has constant reminders of all the bad. Where was I going? Not sure, but I was just going. What was I going to do? Not sure. How was I going to get there? I haven't worked out any details, but I thought I would go to San Francisco and ride my wheelchair down the hill until I get to the bottom. Yeah, not really, but that's how I feel.

I don't know what to do with all these emotions swirling inside me. I feel restless, foggy, angry, and my chest tightens up and it's difficult to breathe, making all this extremely uncomfortable. I lost hope when my wife left me.

How am I going to come back from all this? I was always skeptical about psychiatrist's…they ask a bunch of questions and then give you medicine to help you cope. He can't possibly know what's going on in my head and people believe this stuff. I am not sure about it. I don't want to take meds and then feel like a zombie. I want a doctor to talk with me, not to me."

****

"The right psychiatrist can help you. It's not like what you're thinking. They care and they will help you. Please trust me. I have a friend who is a psychiatrist and I told him all about you and he will be glad to help. He works in a facility which is top notch for behavioral health. He pulled a few strings and got you a bed for when and if you decide to go down this path. I will be there the whole way. Many people have similar troubles, you are not alone. Please remember that. You are never alone. There are many people who hurt. They have come to terms with themselves and now they lead very productive and happy lives, and you can too. Please give it a chance."

"Ok, I'll give it a try…for you."

"No, do it for yourself."

Twelve Months Later

"Happy Anniversary! It has been a year ago today that you started on your journey to better health, happy life, and a great future. How do you Feel?"

"I feel good. I still have a way to go, but I am grateful you stood by me. I understand the process and I am not skeptical anymore. These doctors have a tough job trying to understand behavior in people and what's going on inside their head and then put them on the road to recovery with much success. I have learned a lot this past year. There are a few people who didn't make it through, and that is sad, and I will never forget them. Each step I take will be for them. But there are many people doing very well.

I have a job I like working in the rehab center, and I have been saving for a place of my own. Wheelchair accessible. Physical therapy is going well and although it's a slow process, the doctors are hopeful."

"That's terrific! I knew you could do it. I am so happy for you."

"Thank you. I owe it all to you."

"No, you owe yourself. It's nice to see you smile again."

Silent Isn't Golden

"So, are we all going to keep ignoring what's been going on? No one wants to be the first to end the vortex we found ourselves in. Just eat and run I guess, is that it?"

Glancing around the table, I noticed a few eyes peering up from their dinner plates and a couple eye rolls. Did they hear what I just said? The only response I heard was the sound of the forks hitting the plate harder out of frustration, I'm surprised none of the China was broken.

"Is there no one at this table willing to talk this out and be a family again?"

Phil's ears turn red when he's angry and George looked up a split second and mom stopped eating and placed her fork on her plate looking around for someone to speak.

Whenever we got into trouble when we were kids, while totally ignoring the nannies and babysitters, mom would get frustrated because, one, we were bad, two, she was not home for her to discipline us herself because she was always at the office. But, oh, we would get it bad when she and dad got home. That's the look she had on her face at dinner. The 'you better run' look.

We sat around this dinner table thousands of times before and never have I seen the stone-cold pale expressions like I have these last couple of years. I read the anguish on everyone's faces and I wonder how we became this way. We have always been a normal family...well, what I thought was normal. When you're a kid you think that everyone is the same. Looking back, I realize now that we were not like other people.

We always lived in this mansion built on one hundred acres of land, renovated periodically to keep with modern times whether it needed it or not. Nice cars, the best schools, gourmet meals, the biggest in-ground pool in the neighborhood. We never wanted for anything. Like I said, I thought this was normal.

The company was built by my great-grandfather, Joe when he and his family came to America from Italy. Built it from the ground up with his brains and hard work overcoming all sorts of challenges. It has always been a family business...it was never an option. When we turned sixteen, we worked after school in the mail room until we went off to college...which was their alma mater. We worked in the company during Christmas vacations, spring break, and through the summers until graduation, then we were moved into upper management positions.

Dad passed away a couple of years ago and mom is retired and frail now at eighty and the company falls into the hands of my oldest twin brothers, George and Phil who share ownership and are always fighting. If they aren't arguing about business, they are fighting about who is better, whose kids are more well off and the list goes on.

"What do you want us to say? You gonna play savior little brother?" said Phil.

"I just want to understand everyone's issues, and I do want to save this family from doom. What's wrong with that?" I said.

"Nothing wrong with communication dear," mom said. "I could die happy if this family could get along."

"What's all this fuss about all of a sudden? The company is fine. Everything's fine right?" Emma said.

"Yes, everything is fine. Why wouldn't it be? It's always been fine. Maybe if you show up at the office occasionally you would know what's going on there," said George.

"I'm at the office every day. You're just not paying attention. I know where your attention does go these days, it goes to your assistant and everyone who works in your department," said Jane.

"It does not. I do the work I'm supposed to do and more," said George.

"Yeah, we know the extra work you do. That's why you only hire young women just out of college," said Emma.

"I'm not dead yet," said George.

"You're close," said Jane.

"Shut up!" said George.

"So, this is what you want to talk about?" said Phil. "This petty stuff?"

"No, Phil. I want to talk about why everyone at this table hates each other so much," I said.

"What are you a therapist now? Just leave it be."

"No, this is important," I said. "What happened to this family?"

"What happened to this family is that *some* people at this table are selfish and stubborn," said Jane.

"Don't forget spiteful," said George.

"The only one that's spiteful here is you George," said Jane. "I can't believe you're still mad at me for nothing."

"It's not nothing to me Jane."

"I include you in everything, it's your own fault that you don't insert yourself in things. You don't come over or you cancel at the last minute to hang out with your young chicks. But, regardless, I still invite you," said Jane.

"And I'm tired of covering for you Phil. You drink a lot, you're always hungover, and I am overwhelmed at work. I cannot do my work and your work anymore," said Emma.

"Don't talk to us like you two are perfect angels," said Phil.

"How about those family trips you both take. Or all those "spa" days you two are always going to and let's not forget those hotel bills Jane," George said.

Jane's head burst up and shot imaginary daggers at both George and Phil.

"Yeah, that's right girls. Do you think we didn't know about it? We know it all," said Phil.

The thermostat may say sixty-nine, but it sure feels like eighty-nine in here. Silence covers the room except for utensils slamming the dinner plates and the tension in the dining room is thicker than the pot roast. Everyone's knuckles were red with the tight grip they all had on their forks. No one looked up. I really want to push harder, but it's not going to be easy.

"Earl? Something you want to say?" He poked his head up like he had something to contribute.

"No. No. I uh…nothing to say," Earl said as he wiped the beads of sweat forming on his forehead with the napkin and kept eating like someone set the timer.

"Earl. You know something, don't you," I pressed him again.

"Well…." Earl started.

"Shut your mouth, Earl!"

"No! No, I won't shut up any longer!" Earl said. "I'm tired of all this arguing and I'm tired of all the ruthlessness that goes on at the company and at home. I don't want to be a part of it anymore. You don't care about anyone besides yourselves, you will do anything to make more and more money. I don't see any extra money, the workers don't see anything extra, and Sean here, doesn't see anything so where does all the money go to?! No one wants to work for you. So, go ahead George and Phil, tell them. Tell them everything."

"Earl, I know exactly what you're talking about, except, it's not George or Phil," said mom as she scans the dinner table and sets her eyes on Charlie who has sat through this entire dinner and has said nothing. Everyone's head almost slips off their shoulders when they turn to look at him.

"Tell them Charlie," I said to him. "Tell them how you have been embezzling from our company for years to support your gambling habit. Tell them Charlie. I may be old but I'm not stupid, not by a long shot."

Charlie's face turned bright white. He tried speaking but nothing came out.

"You're caught. It's over now," mom said as everyone's mouth dropped open and heads swiveled between mom's and Charlie's direction.

"Mom, you knew about this?" Jane said.

"Yes, so did Sean," said mom. "Sean, the floor is yours," mom said.

The doorbell rang and Sean got up to answer it. The police enter the foyer and follow Sean to the dining room.

They head straight for Charlie, cuff him, read him his rights and lead him out the door to the police car and drove away.

"What the hell just happened? I don't believe it." said Phil.

"Me neither," said Emma. "Mom, Sean, you both knew? Why didn't you say anything? Why did you let them take Charlie away like that?"

"The D.A. requested it that way. I noticed the books a while ago, went to mom about it and we knew we had to do the right thing," Sean said.

"Wow. So, what happens now?" George asks.

"Charlie will pay his dues and then get the help he needs for his gambling addiction," said Sean.

"We sell the company and be done with it. Don't worry, everyone will be compensated. Everyone will have enough money for yourselves to start their own business or whatever you wish. No more partnerships. You are all on your own. It's time you took care of yourselves and your own families. Then we become a family again," mom said.

"Well, I'm speechless, but I'm for that," said Jane.

"Me too."

"Me too."

"Me too."

It was unbelievable. All that anger seemed to fly away at the idea of selling the company. When great-grandfather started this company, he was a great businessman. Honest and productive. After he passed, somewhere along the way that became the core of the disfunction of this family. The conversations switched from frustration and finger pointing to care and consideration. It was beautiful site. I looked around the table and smiled.

The Gumshoe

The ole Gumshoe Jake Philips was the best of the best detectives with model looks and sharp suits. Some compare him to a modern-day Cary Grant, and they'd be right.

He took to the streets to find the mystery woman he saw in his favorite bar three nights this week drinking expensive wine and dressed to kill. He wanted to approach her but in the blink of an eye she was gone, leaving him to finish his beer solo.

He was astonished that she was able to slip away without him noticing. Jake notices everything…usually. He took a last swig of his beer and ordered another and thought about his next move.

He waved the bartender over to order another beer and to ask him who was the pretty dame that was sitting at the end of the bar just minutes before. Jake has an eye for detail and a nose for trouble. His senses are telling him this beautiful dame is in a mess.

"Don't know her name. Comes in and leaves after having one glass of wine. Always the same time always the same barstool," bartender says.

"What is that time?" He asked him.

"You can set your watch by her. 8PM, for 15 minutes, then leaves. She never meets anyone, never speaks to anyone, and never uses the phone," said Joe the bartender.

"So, she's a regular?"

"Last few weeks," Joe answered as he served another barfly.

Philips is determined to find her. He paid his tab and stepped outside for a smoke thinking of who this woman is. She was tall, with long brown, curly hair, and legs that don't quit.

He planned on coming back tomorrow to offer her his expertise. He was a P.I. after all, and a good one. Philips was a man with a plan.

He called Lucky Lou…his childhood friend. When you're around Lou, you are blessed with good fortune, good friendship, vast knowledge, and remarkable instincts.

Lou is a husky, strong type, and acts as the muscle for Philips. They make a terrific team. With Philips' skill and Lou's karma…that's all he needs.

Philips tossed and turned all night…he couldn't get the mystery woman with the silky, long, brown hair and fancy wine in her hand off his mind. What could she possibly be involved in? This is exactly the kind of case he likes to dig his teeth into.

The next morning, he got dressed and headed to the diner on the corner to meet up with Lou for coffee and a plate full of steak and eggs. No investigation can start on an empty stomach.

Afterwards, they took to the streets asking around if anyone saw their lady in the bar the previous night, but no dice.

Nighttime finally fell and Philips was excited to get to the bar. They arrived early, ordered a couple of beers, took their positions, and waited for the mystery lady.

Philips sat in the furthest corner of the bar while Lou sat at the end of the bar facing the door.

7:56 p.m.

Heart pounding.

Eyes glued to the door. While his eyes were dry from staring, he didn't dare look away for fear of missing her again.

7:58 p.m.

8:00 p.m.

Finally.

8:03 p.m.

A bomb-like sound came from the front of the bar. The door swung open and slammed against the wall. Philips' heart fell when an old man, looking about 96 years old, came in with a big mouth and an odor strong enough to wilt a tulip.

Lou and Philips look at each other with raised hands and a shrug on their shoulders.

8:15 p.m.

What could've happened? Joe the bartender said you can set your clock by her arrival. Did something happen to her? Philips, now more than ever, must find this mystery lady.

Philips and Lou stepped outside and lit up a smoke when they heard a woman screaming from The Elite Hotel across the street. They ran quickly to the hotel and stopped in the lobby and listened.

This hotel is beautiful inside and out. People traveling from all over the country stop here just to say they stayed in *The Elite Hotel*. Marble from floor to ceiling, huge fireplace in the lobby, and complimentary drinks and appetizers for all who enter.

A woman screamed again even louder. Philips and Lou followed the sound of the screams and took off down the hall running ahead of the hotel security stopping at an intersection with heavy breathing…listening for the damsel in distress.

Philips and Lou heard scuffling while standing near room 117, noticed the door was ajar, and heard women's voices arguing. Lou burst passed him into the room and his jaw dropped open.

They couldn't believe what they were seeing. But two women with beautiful brown hair and expensive taste in wine? Only one of them held the gun. But which dame was my mystery lady? Lou looked around for a trick mirror and Philips rubbed his eyes.

Twins? What are the odds? Who is who?

The woman holding the gun…startled…immediately grabbed the hair of the other beauty pulling her in front of herself like a shield swiveling the point of the gun both at us and at her head.

"She's the woman from the bar. The beauty being held," Philips whispered to Lou.

"How do you know? Lou asked.

"Look at how she's dressed. See the difference?" Philips said.

Lou nodded.

The woman in the bar had expensive well-made clothing. The one on the right was made up of hair dye and wanna-be knock-offs. Philips and Lou noticed the difference right away not only in dress but in attitude. Bad attitudes make for ugly people.

"Look, you don't want to hurt her," Philips said.

"Who are you?" She asked.

"Jake Philips, P.I."

"Well, Jake, this isn't any of your business," she said.

"Maybe I can help," Jake said.

"No. You can't help. This is family business. Get out," she said pushing the gun into the woman's temple.

"Give me a chance. I have been known to solve a problem or two," said Jake said.

"Neena wants my emerald," the lady from the bar spurts out.

"Shut up Rhanda!" Neena said.

"Explain to me what happened Neena. I like a fun story," said Jake.

"She has an emerald that belongs to me, and I want it back," Neena said. "Each of us inherited $500,000 cash and an emerald worth $2,000,000 from our grandfather. I took my money and went my own way. My grandfather didn't like my idea of fun, so he gave both emeralds to Rhanda. I need the money and I want it back. It's mine."

"You see, Rhanda was always the good one, always following the rules, she's the one who went to college, started her own business. It's sickening. Hoity toity. All I want is what's mine and I'll be gone. I may even let her live," Neena said.

"I'm sure we can work this out Neena. But not like this. You need to put the gun down so no one gets hurt, and we can come up with a plan," Jake said.

"No. If I give you the gun, you'll jump me, and I go to jail. Either we go all together for the gem, or I shoot her," Neena said.

"Aw hell." Someone said from the hallway.

In a split second the security stormed into the room, voices blazing, and guns drawn. Lou hurled forward towards Neena tackling her to the floor with one hand and knocking the gun away with the other.

I lunged towards Rhanda leading her out of the room. Lou held Neena until the cop's put cuffs on her and took her away.

Rhanda thru her arms around Philips with relief. He returned the favor.

"Hi. I'm Jake Philips. Do you want to have dinner with me?"

"Yes, Jake Philips. I would love it. As long as I can have a glass of wine with dinner."

They both smiled.

The Humble Award

"Good evening, ladies, gentlemen, and the youth of our community. Most of you know me and for those of you who may not know me, I'm Steve Glendall. I am this year's Chairman of the Youth and Community Guidance Committee. But it's not about me. I am surrounded by good-hearted people who come together to help lift each other's spirits in any way they can.

The Humble Award has always stood for prestige, compassion, tenaciousness, and honor. Well, the recipients of this year's Humble Award are all these things and more. They are selfless and go above and beyond to help others when it is needed. Let me tell you a few things about our extraordinary friends.

They get their hands dirty. When the Walters family was having trouble selling their house, they went over and helped them conquer the clutter, paint the inside of the house, and do landscaping to make the house look pretty.

When old lady Estelle Jones passed away at the age of 97, it was found that she didn't have money for her own funeral, nor did she have a will or life insurance. Estelle's family was small and had passed away years before, and she was the last surviving member. So, they put together a benefit to help reimburse the funeral home and any final expenses she left behind.

They volunteer at the local youth center. Unfortunately, there are more troubled and homeless youths than there are volunteers. These days life is remarkably busy for most, but we are lucky to have our friends in our community who dedicate their retirement years to our young kids. They make them feel loved, welcome, and guide them for a successful future. Our youngsters love and respect them in return, and they work hard to please them.

If someone is sick, they will visit, if someone needs a ride somewhere, they will drive them, and when there are ball games playing, they will be there to cheer them on.

They don't do it for notoriety, nor do they do it for gratitude. They do it because they love it. They love people, they love this community, and they love seeing people happy and succeed. You see, they know they have been truly fortunate in their lives, blessed family, successful careers, beautiful home…they wanted to give back. Frankly, I don't know what our town would do without them.

So, I know you are tired of listening to me and would rather hear from our favorite people.

Laughter.

So, without further ado, I would like to introduce to you the winners of this year's Humble Award…Mr. and Mrs. Andrew and Jean Caldarini!"

Applause and standing ovation.

"Thank you. Thank you all," says Andrew. "We are overwhelmed. When Steve stopped by our house a couple of days ago and told Jean and I we were this year's winner of the Humble Award, I asked him if he had been drinking. His reply was, "not on a school night."

Laughter

"I told him…we don't do what we do for any kind of award. We do it to give back."

Jean says, "we have been very blessed in our lives, and we want others to feel the same. We want others to know they can have as many blessings as possible and more in their lives too. When we came here to retire in Turlington, we loved it, but we were surprised at the countless people here were only existing and not living and how many others including young kids needed help and guidance with education and life ethics."

"So, Jean and I decided to be involved. Our town where we were born, lived, and raised our family was so incredibly good to us that we wanted to pay it forward. Both of us are in good health and have a fairly good sense of life since we are older than most. We hoped that our life experiences could help others. We saw people struggle and it broke our hearts, so we step in when we are able."

"It keeps us busy and our minds sharp and at our age, that's a big deal," Jean says.

Laughter

"We have gotten to know everyone in this community and think of you all as our family…a very big family…who we care about and love," says Jean. "We see you happy and that makes us happy. We do not do this for the adoration, although that's a great perk."

Andrew steps in and says, "I want to tell you a little story. Shortly after we moved to Turlington, Jean and I were taking a walk, getting to know the neighborhood, and we found ourselves at the park and kept walking through. Along our path, we came across two young boys, Jack who was eight years old, and Michael who was ten years old at the time. They were on the swings, but they weren't swinging. They were sitting with their heads hanging down, and tears in their eyes.

Jean and I looked around for a mom or dad but the only people we saw were other kids at the far end of the playground, but their moms and dads were nearby. We thought they were lost, we got concerned, and we cautiously approached them staying a couple of feet away not to scare them by getting too close.

After talking to them a bit, Jack and Michael had recently lost their father who they missed terribly but also, the dad promised to buy them a new basketball hoop for their driveway. Their mom had told them they couldn't afford it for a while, and she would have to get a better job just to make ends meet. Of course, this was upsetting to the boys, yet understandable from the mom's point.

We asked them to walk with Jean and I to show us where they lived, which was close by. The playground was near their backyard and mom, Jackie, came outside and thanked us for watching out for her boys.

The next day, Jean and I went to Walmart, bought a basketball hoop, and brought it to Jack and Michael. I can't tell you how happy that made them. The look on Jack and Michael's faces lit up like a sunrise at early morning. Jackie cried saying she couldn't possibly pay us back, but we told her it was our gift.

We stayed the rest of the day. Jack, Michael, and I put the hoop together and Jean helped Jackie inside the house. From that day on we looked out for the boys, and all became a family. Now

Jack is graduating from college and Michael is a CPA at a firm in the next town over. Jackie, Jean, and I couldn't be prouder.

So, it was the look on those boys' faces and the help we were able to give the family that is why we do this work. Not for the prestige, not for awards, and not for the thank you given back to us. It's for the smiles."

"Jack, Michael, and Jackie, stand up," Jean says.

They stand as applause sounds the room.

"Andrew and I aren't sure we deserve such praise, because we love smiles, happiness, and the people," says Jean.

"Thank you." "Thank You"

Cheers and applause

Welcome to the Neighborhood

Molly Drake stepped out in the middle of the street to take a picture of her new house to email her family and friends back home. She doesn't live far, but she is so excited to have a house of her own, she couldn't wait to send them pictures.

It's a beautiful home inside and out, only ten years old and well-built in a wonderful neighborhood. Lovely pale-yellow siding with a colorful brick laid driveway leading to her two-car garage and a pebble walkway leading to the front door.

Molly moved into her new house yesterday and is excited to get things unpacked and in place so she can venture out and meet her new neighbors. This is the first time Molly is out on her own and feels blessed to have a fantastic job that she loves as a pharmacist in one of the biggest drug stores in the tri-state area. She worked hard to get this far and has mentally made plans for her future.

After a long day, Molly decided to relax early, so she made herself a delicious chicken Caesar salad and poured herself a glass of her favorite white wine. She sat down and took one bite of salad, and the doorbell rang.

She put her fork on the plate and headed toward the door as she finished chewing her salad, she looked through the peep hole…staring back at her was a wine bottle and holding it was a woman with a fancy short haircut, the figure of a model, and a fresh acrylic manicure.

Then she opened the front door.

"Hi! I'm Celeste Beaumont…I live directly across the street from you in the white Victorian. I brought you wine to welcome you to the neighborhood. I thought we can get to know each other."

"Oh, how nice of you. Thank you very much. I'm Molly Drake," she said as she took the wine from Celeste. "Please come in."

"Thank you very much," she said as Molly shut the door. "Oh, I'm sorry, am I interrupting your dinner?"

"It's only a chicken Caesar salad, in fact I made a large bowl, would you like some?"

"Yes, that sounds great. I'm all for healthy eating. Have you met any of our other neighbors yet?" Celeste said as she put the wine bottle on the dining room table.

"No. I have not had a chance yet. You're the first one."

"Good. I like being the first. I have a feeling we can become close friends," Celeste said with a crooked smile.

"So, Molly, what do you do for a living?"

"I'm a pharmacist. I work at Reese Pharma."

"Oh, that's wonderful. Congratulations. I'm a hairstylist and the owner of Hair For You Salon."

"Oh, great. I am not a fancy person, but I do appreciate a good haircut."

"Of course. Let me know and I'll put you into my schedule."

Molly got another plate and utensils and a wine glass and opened the bottle Celeste brought. They went on to have a wonderful conversation while they finished dinner. Celeste washed the dishes while Molly dried and put them away. They refilled their wines glasses and sat in the living room on Molly's new couch to continue their conversation.

Molly was having a fun time. She met someone she felt she could be longtime friends with. But Molly's eyes were weighing heavy suddenly…she began yawning.

"Molly are you alright?"

"I'm sorry Celeste, I had a long day unpacking and I guess I had too much wine. The combination is weighing on me. I think we should call it a night," she said as she continued to yawn but never made it off the couch…she was out cold.

Molly awakens to darkness. She glances out the window to see the moonlight shining through the windows and the sound of crickets chirping. A dimly lit lamp is glowing in the living room and a soft shining nightlight over the sink in the kitchen. Confused…she looked at the clock near the TV…9:34 p.m. How could she have slept this long?

Molly jolted upright, her pupils widened, and her jaw fell open…shock whittled through her body.

"Oh, you're awake. I made us dinner. You must be famished by now."

"Celeste?"

"Oh, no, dear. My name is Molly."

"I'm Molly. Why are you dressed in my clothes? And your hair…it's exactly like mine."

"I don't understand, dear. These are my clothes, and this is my natural hair."

Molly looks up at Celeste and is speechless. She stands up and looks her directly in the eye, "Celeste, what do you think you are doing?"

"My name is not Celeste, dear. My name is Molly. *You* are Celeste. You live across the street, and you came over with a bottle of wine to welcome me to the neighborhood. We had a genuinely nice lunch and you fell asleep on my couch from all that wine," she says. "Oh, my. That wine sure did mess with your head."

Molly's forehead wrinkles…she opened her mouth to talk but no words came out. Celeste looked just like her. She is wearing her clothes, walking the same way as Molly, talking the same, and she even has her hair the same way as Molly has hers.

"Would you like some chicken Caesar salad and some wine? I made too much. We can get to know each other better," she says as she takes Molly's arm to lead her to the dining room table, but Molly pulls angrily away. Celeste grabs her arm again.

"I said to sit, and I will get you salad," Celeste says authoritatively.

"Celeste, you're crazy. What do you think you will get out of this?" Molly's lips pursed in frustration. She closed her eyes and sighed, wondering if this was real.

Celeste comes back with two salad plates and utensils which she sets on the table and returns to the kitchen to bring a bottle of wine and two wine glasses and sets them beside the salad plates. Before she sits, she pours the wine.

"So Celeste, tell me about yourself," she says.

"Stop calling me Celeste! *You* are Celeste. *I* am Molly!"

"Here, dear. Drink your wine, you will feel better," she says.

Molly gulps the glass of wine, hoping that if she passed out again, she would wake up and everything will be back to normal. This is the weirdest thing she has ever been into. She slides her empty glass towards Celeste for her to refill it with more wine.

"Whoa. Take it easy dear, you'll pass out again. You need to eat," Celeste said.

Molly takes the glass and gulps that down as well as the next one. Beginning to get sleepy, she goes to the couch, lays down, and she fell asleep…again.

Molly woke up and it was still pitch dark outside, the only lamp on was the one in the living room, and the clock said 9:34pm. She hops off the couch and looks around to notice Celeste in

Molly's same clothes, in the kitchen making the same chicken Caesar salad and the same bottle of wine on the counter near her.

"Oh, you're awake. I made us dinner. You must be famished by now."

"Celeste! Please stop this right now. Stop this ridiculous charade you put me in," says Molly.

"Oh, no, dear. My name is Molly."

"No! No, it's not! *You* are Celeste!"

"My name is not Celeste, dear. My name is Molly. *You* are Celeste. You live across the street, and you came over with a bottle of wine to welcome me to the neighborhood. We had a genuinely nice lunch and you fell asleep on my couch from all that wine," she says. "Oh, my. That wine sure did mess with your head."

"This is ridiculous," said Molly.

"Have some salad dear, I made too much."

Molly knew she had to stop this strange life recycling she is in, but she doesn't know how. She decided to sit and eat the salad and drink the wine while she thought about what to do.

"So Celeste, tell me about yourself," she says. "Here, dear. Drink your wine, you will feel better," she says.

Molly drinks repeatedly, hoping that she will fall asleep and wake up and things will be normal again. She didn't know what else to do. Before long, Molly zonked out on the couch…again.

The phone rings and startles Molly, she jumps into a sitting position to answer it. She looks around her bedroom quizzically as she talks.

"Yea, hi mom. Yea, I'm fine. Everything is just great. I love my new house. I love you too," she says as she hangs up the phone.

****

Molly climbed out of bed and immediately went to the window, opened the curtains, and looked outside in relief. The sun was shining brightly on a beautiful day. She exited her bedroom cautiously and slowly stepped downstairs while looking all over for her neighbor Celeste, but she wasn't there.

Molly entered the kitchen, and it was clean…left the same as when she left it the night before, or what she thinks was the night before. She opens the refrigerator and notices the extra salad she made is in a bowl on the shelf and what's left in the bottle of wine she opened is on the bottom shelf. The dining room table was clean, and the couch was neat showing no signs that Molly slept on

She exhaled a huge sigh of relief, that it all had to be a weird dream.

The doorbell rings.

Molly froze.

The doorbell rings again.

Molly looks through the peephole, gasps, and jumps back. She opens the door about six inches.

"Hi! I'm Celeste Beaumont…I live directly across the street from you in the white Victorian. I brought you wine to welcome you to the neighborhood. I thought we can get to know each other."

76

77

78

79

Made in the USA
Middletown, DE
19 March 2024

51565388R00044